Other Bo

(Available through the p

PRAYERS AND RITUALS
  Prayers for a Planetary Pilgrim
  Prayers for the Domestic Church
  Prayers for the Servants of God
  Psalms for Zero Gravity

PARABLES AND STORIES
  The Gospel of Gabriel
  The Quest for the Flaming Pearl
  St. George and the Dragon
  The Magic Lantern
  The Ethiopian Tattoo Shop
  Sundancer
  The Christmas Eve Storyteller
  Little Orphan Angela
  The Passionate Troubadour

CONTEMPORARY SPIRITUALITY
  The Pilgrimage Way of the Cross
  Prayer Notes to a Friend
  The Great Escape Manual
  The Ladder
  The Old Hermit's Almanac
  The Lenten Labyrinth
  The Lenten Hobo Honeymoon
  Holy Fools & Mad Hatters
  A Pilgrim's Almanac
  Pray All Ways
  Secular Sanctity
  In Pursuit of the Great White Rabbit
  The Ascent of the Mountain of God
  Feathers on the Wind
  The Lenten Pharmacy
  Embrace the Healing Cross
  Make Straight the Crooked Ways

© 2006 by Edward M. Hays

www.forestofpeace.com

International Standard Book Number: 0-939516-76-4

Cover and interior art by Edward M. Hays

Cover and text design by Kristen Burt

Printed and bound in the United States of America.

Preface

A prescription was originally a written order by a physician to a pharmacist to create a medicine for a particular ailment by the grinding and mixing of various drugs. The following prayscriptions present the opportunity for you to be your own pharmacist, so as to prepare medicines for the wellness of your spirit and heart. Some are prayers, others are helpful hints for holy living, and still others are brief meditations. Instead of grinding and pounding, these prayscriptions require prayerful pondering and mixing them into your daily life. These medications are designed to treat spirit and body as a united reality. Your soul is not a visiting guest. It intimately vitalizes each cell and atom of your body so that whatever heals the spirit produces beneficial effects in the body as well.

Lent is a very ancient medication, dating back to the third and fourth centuries. It was originally a treatment lasting one or two weeks, but with time it became a therapy lasting some forty days. The original prescription for this forty-day medication included harsh penances and abstaining from all flesh meat and all things that come from flesh, such as milk, cheese, eggs, and butter. Today Lent isn't so severe, but it remains medicinal.

The pharmacy symbol "Rx," found on prescriptions and used in the following pages, is a symbolic abbreviation of the Latin *recipere,* meaning "take thou." As you take to heart the following prayscriptions, may you find them healing.

Ash Wednesday

As Lent begins today, recall that Jesus said his mission was to the sick, and not those in good health. So ask yourself, "How do I feel?" If your answer is "comfortable," you may suffer from *comfyitis,* a lethal disease of the spirit that requires the bitter medicine of discomfort—an itchy dissatisfaction with one's self, with how you pray, and with how you live the gospel. Discomfort heals by producing the craving to become a seeker of daring ways to improve yourself.

Rx: Gracious God,
 Since seekers seek, make me a lenten
  searcher
 who, in pursuit of you, departs from
  the comfortable,
 setting forth on an adventurous
  forty-day expedition
 of prayer, discipline, and the desire to find
  you afresh.

St. Francis of Assisi is reported to have said, "What you are looking for is what is looking for you." Finding a cure for *comfyitis* doesn't require making a pilgrimage to the Holy Land or a local monastery since what you're seeking is seeking you! Paradoxically, the cure is simply this: Sit still and be fully present to wherever you are. Be patient; empty yourself of all expectations or illusions of how the Sacred Mystery who is seeking you will appear.

Rx: O Wearer of Endless Disguises,
　　　Your arrival outside of sacred zones
　　　　　isn't announced
　　　by ringing little silver bells
　　　　　or loud thunderclaps.
　　　Come, cleanse my eyes
　　　　　so that I may recognize you
　　　in your beloved secular attire.

Friday after Ash Wednesday

In the Buddhist tradition there is a story of a man who daily hunted rabbits in a forest. One day a rabbit ran right past him and collided with a tree stump, knocking itself unconscious. "A gift from the gods!" the hunter shouted as he picked up the rabbit and put it in his hunting sack. For the rest of his life, he came every day to that very same place in the forest, and sat down watching that stump, waiting for it to happen again.

Rx: God says to us:
    "Search not for me in expected places;
    I rarely return to the scene of the crime.
    Use extreme caution, and always handle
    ordinary stuff like a ticking time bomb,
    ready to burst open with unexpected
    gifts."

Saturday after Ash Wednesday

Examine yourself for some of the symptoms of *comfyitis*: your material situation is too secure, your life's too comfortable and pleasurable, religiously you feel contented. *Comfyitis* prevents true discipleship since every student, as the Teacher said, must repent and become a lifelong convert.

The drug discomfort acts as an agitator of a complacent heart that is resistant to change. Self-satisfaction creates narcolepsy, while self-righteousness anesthetizes conversion. So, find healing by happily embracing uncomfortable confrontations, homilies, or whatever else awakens you to an urgent need to change.

Rx: Gentle God,
   Smug souls suffer sleeping sickness.
   Awaken me to live in endless discontent,
   not with what I have, but with who I am.

First Sunday in Lent

When Jesus the Seeker goes into the desert on retreat, we are not told if he finds God, only that the devil finds him! The Koran relates how Lucifer, the Angel of Light, is going to seek revenge on God after his fall from heaven. Satan tells God, "I will waylay your servants as they walk on your straight path, then spring upon them from the front and from the rear, from the right and from their left."

So if you're walking the straight path, observing all the commandments, and devoutly attending church—beware!

Rx: Merciful God,
    Teach me to walk the straight path,
    humbly cautious yet joyfully certain
    that each temptation isn't a death trap,
    but rather a disguised invitation to love.

Spiritual reading is a classic lenten exercise, but read with caution! Spiritual literature can easily entertain only the mind while being impotent to arouse one to conversion. For reading to be nutritious, read slowly and always digest what you've read. A book can be a good spiritual guide when it challenges the reader to dare to tread new paths, to expand, or even to discard previous beliefs. Take heart if you're searching for such a guidebook: when the reader is ready, the book will appear.

Rx: One sentence is all I need to chew upon,
and then digest it into the stuff of my life.

Tuesday of the First Week

The great commandment of loving God and your neighbor as yourself requires, first of all, a wholesome love of yourself. A prescription for such a good self-love is to develop an openness to criticism and an eagerness to acknowledge your mistakes. Add generosity in the giving of compliments and being comfortable in receiving them. Next, cultivate curiosity and openness to new ideas and experiences, along with a flexibility and playfulness in responding to unexpected situations. Finally, habitually practice the healing humor of laughing aloud at your self.

Rx: O Divine Midwife,
    Enlighten me to the value of criticism and
        praise,
    twin-inspired sources of information for
        excellence.
    Daily spur me on in being my own
        best critic
    so that I can accomplish
        my original birthing blueprint.

Wednesday of the First Week

The most prominent lenten symbol is the cross, and the Jerusalem cross is an ancient sign of healing protection. The horizontal line of a Jerusalem cross bisects the vertical line in the middle, and at the end of each line is a small cross. The four crosses grafted onto a large cross represent the principle of defending every entrance with a barrier, and so was a potent prophylactic to ward off evil and pestilence. If you find yourself in need or in danger, pray the following with outstretched arms:

Rx: Cross on my left, cross on my right,
  cross over my head, cross beneath my feet:
  banish pestilence and protect me from
  harm.

Thursday of the First Week

Ancient pharmacies, like modern drugstores, offered eye shadow cosmetics. Egyptian pharmacists prescribed the use of blue eye shadow to ward off the sun, protect the wearer from the Evil Eye, and to enhance the beauty of the eyes. For those seeking beautiful eyes—both males and females—there is this flawless prescription: Look upon others with love and kindness, and consciously allow your luminous spirit to sparkle in your eyes.

Rx: O my eyes, be flowing faucet sacraments, pouring forth my love upon all you see: friend, stranger, family, or foe alike.

Friday of the First Week

Blindness was common in the ancient Near East because of the sun's intensity, blowing dust, and the lack of cleanliness. But even without these harsh conditions, you can suffer from a blinding eye infection: bias. The source of this blindness is the disease of thinking negative, prejudicial thoughts. The cure for it is the reverse medicine: the thinking of "positive," prejudicial thoughts. Healing is found by thinking about how your world is so vastly enhanced by the rich variety of persons of different colors, nations, social status, political positions, and religious beliefs. If for any reason you find this too difficult to swallow, ponder the following:

Rx: The Greeks said, "Often the gods visit us
    as strangers."
The gods—unwashed, immoral, poor,
    and homeless?
Yes, but the ancient Greeks were only half
    right:
not often, but always, does God visit us
    in the stranger.

16

Saturday of the First Week

The compelling sense of God's absence in our world can easily fester into spiritual skepticism and troubling doubts of God's existence. Treat this condition by practicing the sixth sense of the saints: absence. In God's *unpresence* find the Divine presence. *Unpresence* is a very tangible and real presence, as those whose life partner has died will tell you. About their homes and in their lives they sense the *unpresence* of their deceased beloved.

Rx: While I cannot see, hear, taste, smell, or
        feel you,
      in your seeming absence I sense
        your presence.

Second Sunday of Lent

Today is Striptease Sunday when Jesus' flesh becomes transparent, allowing the luminous presence within to shine forth. What was true for the transfigured Jesus is also true for us. Like clouds that hide the sun on an overcast day, your flesh conceals the awesome splendor of the Divine. To daily live out your stunning interior radiance is truly transfiguring.

Rx: Open your pores; let your light shine out.
    Glow in the dark and light up the gloom.
    Vow that you'll never know a cloudy day,
    being nightlessly the light of the world.

Monday of the Second Week

"You know the time in which we are living," Paul admonished the Romans—and the Americans (Rom 13:11). "It is now the hour for you to wake from sleep." After such a rousing wake-up call, the reason why so many are still napping after two millennia may be found in slowly chewing on this Jewish parable:

Rx: There once was a Russian village so poor that it did not have a single clock. But the people wanted to know the time of day, and begged their villager elders to meet their need. After much pondering, the wise elders had their village carpenter build a sundial. Oh, what a work of art it was! But one day a thunderstorm came, and the villagers cried, "Our beautiful sundial is getting wet, it will be ruined!" After three days of deliberation the wise elders ordered the carpenter to build a roof over the sundial.

Tuesday of the Second Week

Tension is a common affliction at work, in traffic, and at home created by contemporary life's hectic pace. If you are a tension sufferer and seek relief, take the following medicine: Upon becoming aware of being tense, take three deep breaths or, better yet, simply yawn. Dr. Tubesing of the Whole Person Association says a good yawn gives total release from tension.

Rx: Yawning in church, at work, and at home is healthy since, like bats, deadly tensions fly out your mouth, leaving behind untangled knots in your gut and soul.

"Trying to hang on to youth, trying to hang on to what was really great twenty years ago, throws you totally off," says the scholar of myth, Joseph Campbell. "You've got to . . . seek the abundance that's in the new thing. If you hang on to the old thing, you will not experience the new." Jesus said he wanted to give us life in great abundance, so heed Campbell's warning that in clinging to the old, you'll miss the abundance found in the new.

Rx: Alas, all too easily, I prefer the old to the new;
clinging to threadbare and pious antiques.

God of Passion,
loosen my grip so that I can have new life in abundance!

21

Thursday of the Second Week

Our lenten quest to find God in unexpected places is an inseparable activity from viewing everything as sacred and seeing common things as sacramental. To make vacuuming the carpet, doing the laundry, or grocery shopping a sacrament sometimes requires beginning these activities with a prayer. A simpler way is to use this priestly prescription for consecration: "Love whatever you do!" Performing the daily parade of ordinary tasks with love transforms them—and you--into living prayers.

Rx: Love consecrates the common into the
    sacred,
   making everything it touches into a
    sacrament,
     saturating all things with God's
     presence.

Friday of the Second Week

Jesus says, "From everyone to whom much has been given, much will be required" (Lk 12:48). This saying is usually understood as a call to be productively responsible for our gifts of money, talents, and grace. Yet gifts are given for the enjoyment of the receiver, so, along with productivity, examine yourself on your enjoyment of them. Gratitude is a medicinal grace. So, for any failure to delight and take pleasure in your gifts, make this a lenten Thanksgiving Day.

Rx: Let me list my gifts, rejoicing in each
      one by one,
   since on my personal Easter, the Lord of
      Surprises may ask me:
      "Beloved, did you enjoy my gifts?"

Saturday of the Second Week

"They say stress is a killer," the actress Helen Hayes said, "but I think no stress is equally deadly, especially as you get older. If your days just seem to slip by without any highs or lows, without some anxieties and pulse-quickening occurrences, you may not be really living."

Daily stressful difficulties are often called "life's little crosses." Transform them by renaming them "life's little *Red* Crosses"—healing help for a full life.

Rx: Entertain life's inevitable stresses.
    Take delight in short-lived attacks of
        tension as vital ingredients
    of life's roller-coaster ride,
    as health insurance for living more than
        half a life.

Third Sunday of Lent

A parallel parable to the Good Samaritan is the lenten gospel of the Bad Samaritan (Jn 4:5–42). Jesus, tired and thirsty, is resting alone by Jacob's well outside a Samaritan town when a local woman comes to draw water. Contrary to religious custom, he, a man, engages an unescorted woman in conversation. As a devout Jew, he becomes unclean by contact with a Samaritan, who would have been seen as a heretic. She was no Good Samaritan either. As Jesus points out, she has had five husbands and is now living with a sixth man.

Rx: Heal me, O parable of the Bad Samaritan.
    Cure my crooked eyesight of looking down
    upon others because of their sexual
        behavior.
    Give me the eyes of Jesus which saw only
        good.

Monday of the Third Week

T. S. Eliot in his *Murder in the Cathedral* writes,
"Men fear fire and men fear flood and men fear
pestilence; but more than anything else they fear
the love of God."

Rx: Spare me, O God, your great love and
    affection,
    if an example of one you loved is Jesus on
      Calvary!
    Love me, but leave me alone and stay far,
      far away,
    lest you ask of me that I also do impossible
      things.

Tuesday of the Third Week

Buddha prescribed, "Live in joy, in health, even among the afflicted." Implied in his next words is the health to which he referred: "Live in joy, in love, even among those who hate."

How easily we can misjudge the hostile atmosphere of a gathering, our workplace, or some situation, instead of correctly seeing it as being infected with the most deadly of contagions: hatred. As such, the people involved need healing, not judgment.

Rx: Most Compassionate One,
   Inoculate me with your holy peace and
      courage,
   that I may be healthy among the stressful
      and fearful.
   Immunize me with your deep serenity
      and fulfillment,
   so I can be well among the fearful
      and discontented.

As a friend of mine watches the darkness of night disappear with the coming of dawn, he asks, "Where does the dark go when my eyes are full of light?" The answer to this Zen-like riddle may be found in pondering this rabbinical story:

Rx: A disciple of the famous Maggid of Mezerich was a holy rabbi named Reb Zusia, who was gifted with clairvoyant powers. Once, when a man came to visit his teacher and Zusia was present, he suddenly exposed the visitor's secret acts of dishonesty and deceit. Zusia, feeling guilty for shaming his teacher's visitor, begged his mentor for a blessing. From that day onward he became blind to the evil of others, even if someone sinned right in front of him. He saw only the good in others, and even if someone did something truly evil, he experienced it as his own wrongdoing.

Where did all this darkness go? Did the rabbi's eyes—being filled with light absorb the darkness and convert it into light?

Thursday of the Third Week

The Swiss phychiatrist Carl Jung warned physicians that their patients would more willingly accept the skeletons in the closets of their unconscious than they would the gold hidden there. Fear makes us non-believers of our God-given potential, of our inherent design to be God's holy instruments.

Rx: Creator of all good things,
My closet skeletons don't frighten me,
for if exposed, they'll cause only disgrace.
Terrifying within me is your hidden gold,
for by using it, I shall become full of grace.

Friday of the Third Week

A good talk is curative since it is therapeutic to talk about your problems with someone who can listen, even if she or he isn't a professional. When inviting a guest into their homes, the Inuit natives of Canada say, "Speak, so that I may see you." Within each of us are aspects of ourselves that we are unable to recognize, but when we speak about them we bring them into the light where we can see and acknowledge them.

Rx: Want to talk, but can't find anyone to
   listen?
Talk aloud to yourself—and listen
   carefully.
Or speak with the silent tongue
   of your pen on paper;
you will find that you can see far more
   of you.

Saturday of the Third Week

A frightening proverb says, "Every generation has to have a war!" The history of the past hundred years seems to point to the truth of that saying. About every twenty years or so a war has broken out in the world. Wars temporarily purge the dark, ungodly shadow side of our culture and ourselves.

G. K. Chesterton said that it is incorrect to speak of war breaking out, as war is the normal state of the world. More correctly, we should speak of peace breaking out.

Rx: Jesus sought to cure us of the pestilence of
    war,
    not by the medicine of war, but by
       eradicating its causes:
       anger, violent thoughts, hateful speech.
    To end war: Frequently wash your hands
       and your heart of these contagions.

Fourth Sunday of Lent

Saliva is a prehistoric healing medicine. If we accidentally cut a finger we instinctively lick it. The Physician of Nazareth made use of this primeval prescription as he mixed his saliva with dust, making a paste to smear on the eyes of a man blind since birth (John 9:14).

Be your own pharmacist today. Mix a faith-filled prayer with some of your saliva and apply this ageless medicine on blind, prejudiced eyes or a bruised heart.

Rx: As I've licked my finger to turn a page,
  I now lick my finger to turn away a pain.
  Physician of Nazareth,
  nurse me back to health.

Monday of the Fourth Week

Isaiah quotes God as saying, "For a brief moment I abandoned you . . . ." (Is 54:7).

On Good Friday, Jesus questioned whether God had turned a deaf ear to his prayers and abandoned him. Who among us has not also experienced the same kind of seemingly God-forsaken moments? These are not fleeting moments, but ones that seem to drag on and on, as did the agony of Jesus on the cross. At these times, pray like this:

Rx: Hurry up, Lord;
    end this moment of seeming
      abandonment.
    Not for moments, but for months it seems
      you have forsaken me.
    I ache to personally experience your next
      words to Isaiah,
    ". . . then, with great tenderness,
      I will take you back."

Tuesday of the Fourth Week

Saluting is a military ritual where the right hand is raised to touch the cap. The term "salute" was once used for any salutation, like tipping one's hat, bowing, or greeting another. To greet another is the most blessed of all wishes. It is a wish of good health, since the Latin mother word of salute is *salus,* which means "health."

Rx: "Hello" is no simple, polite greeting, but a healing wish.
So, pole-vault over politeness to prayerfulness,
filling every greeting with holy, healing grace.

Wednesday of the Fourth Week

Medical science has given some people who were born blind the ability to see. Many who are so healed report experiencing traumatic shock when they first behold the awesome beauty of creation. A few find the gift of vision so unbearable as to request that the operation be reversed! Babies cannot see clearly for quite some time lest they be overwhelmed by the grandeur of all that swirls around them.

If whatever you are looking at today appears dull and ordinary, consider praying as did blind Bartimaeus of Jericho, "My teacher, let me see again!" (Mk 10:51).

Rx: My to-do list for today is truly
    insignificant.
  What really matters is trying to see the
    grandeur of life.
  Dare me to squint, so I can see but a teeny
    bit of it!

Thursday of the Fourth Week

Assisting the poor is an act of justice, not pity! While legally we have ownership of our money, in reality we are only managers of it. God's theory of wealth is found in Psalm 24: "The earth is the Lord's and all that is in it." This clearly states that *everything* belongs to God! As managers of our wealth, justice requires that we wisely dispose of it according to the wishes of its rightful owner, mindful that a day is coming when all managers will be audited!

Rx: A prayscription for shrewd managers:

> Turn my head around, O God, so I can
>   think correctly.
> Heal the erroneous idea—
>   a cousin to "the world is flat"—
> that "my money belongs to me to do with
>   as I like!"

36

Friday of the Fourth Week

Nichola Coddington wrote of desiring a compassion-meter that could indicate the suffering an object had caused on its way to her. Just imagine if you had such a handheld compassion-meter: You could pass over the food on your plate or articles of clothing you are about to buy after learning of the suffering endured by others so that you could have an enjoyable meal or an inexpensive garment. Such an instrument would likely be outlawed for causing emotional distress and massive boycotts!

Impotency is painful. To be conscious of the suffering endured for our comfort, yet to be powerless to relieve it because of the complexities of global economies, would indeed be painful. Yet pain is useful when it acts as nature's alarm for the presence of disease and evil. Do not readily avoid it!

Rx: O wounded Healer, make me
  compassionate,
 so as to feel the suffering of those who
  produce whatever I eat,
   wear, or use—
 even if I feel impotent in relieving it.

37

Arabs have a beautiful custom of a host sharing salt with guests at a meal. This salt-sharing creates a sacred bond or covenant between host and guest. When you share salt with another, the Salt Covenant says you are forbidden to speak ill of or do any harm to the other. The incorruptibility of salt is a sign of perpetuity, and so salt-sharers express their desire that their friendship be long lasting. Even God's long lasting fidelity is pledged to us ". . . by a covenant of salt." (2 Chr 13:5).

Rx: Praying meal blessings in public places is difficult.
But, no need to bow heads, close eyes, and whisper.
Just silently share salt, sprinkled in your palms,
blessing a meal and friendship in an old, salty ritual.

38

Fifth Sunday of Lent

Informed that his friend Lazarus was dying, Jesus says, "This illness does not lead to death; rather it is for God's glory" (Jn 11:3). He restored Lazarus to life and also performed a twin restoration for the woman about to be stoned to death for adultery. The grandeur of God's compassionate pardon was revealed in her being set free from her terminal sickness of soul. Facing her righteous accusers who were so eager to condemn her to death, the physician Jesus scribbles in the dirt a prescription for them—and for us:

Rx: Never judge another for their moral
failures,
lest God, who knows your every hidden
sin,
condemn you for them—and your
hypocrisy.

Monday of the Fifth Week

Slavery was a repulsive reality at the time of Jesus, yet he never condemned it. Among the early converts to Christianity were both slaveholders and their slaves. St. Paul admonished baptized slaves: "Were you a slave when called? Do not be concerned about it. For whoever was called in the Lord as a slave is a freed person belonging to the Lord, just as whoever was free when called is a slave of Christ . . . do not become slaves of human masters" (1 Cor 7:21–23).

The apostolic admonition not to become slaves of others is addressed to each of us who so easily are enslaved to those in authority, to other's opinions, and to a host of major and minor addictions.

Rx: Be free in heart and spirit; defy all who
        try to enslave you
        by power or intimidation.
    Shackles can only bind minds
        —never hearts!

Tuesday of the Fifth Week

Did Jesus die of a stroke? The medical meaning of a stroke is an apoplectic seizure, a sudden blockage or rupture of a blood vein in the brain. The original meaning of a stroke was "to have been struck down by God." In ancient times, sicknesses, especially sudden attacks like strokes, were viewed as divine retribution for sins. Medieval medical books prescribed specific treatments for "the stroke of God's hand." Was it by a stroke of God's hand (or will) that Jesus was crucified, or was he struck down by the hands of the Temple and that of the Roman Empire because he was living out God's radical vision of love and justice?

Rx: O God, whom Jesus said to call "Our
  Father,"
 confirm my faith that you never strike
  down with cancer or crucifixion
  your beloved children,
 but daily stroke us with your loving
  affection.

Wednesday of the Fifth Week

Lent is for sinners, but you say you keep all the commandments. While that is praiseworthy, reflect on these words of Jesus, "just as you did not do it to one of the least of these, you did not do it to me" (Mt 25:45). Then ponder these words of the Jewish Talmud, "Whoever is able to protest against the transgressions of the world and does not is responsible for the transgressions of the entire world!"

Do a soul-search for your involvement in the sins of corporations and of America, as well as the exploitation of Jesus in the less fortunate in your daily life—transgressions for which you voice no protest.

Rx: Lent is purging time.
    So cleanse me, O my Lord.
  Have pity on me. Flush out all my
    transgressions,
  especially my silence in the face of
    injustice.

Jesus warned us that it was risky to follow him. The Italian motion picture director Federico Fellini said, "One of the greatest handicaps is to fear to make a mistake." He said you can't wait for the perfect situation or moment, proclaiming that it is better to make a mistake of action rather than one of inaction.

Rx: Lord, I'm guilty of grievous sins of
        omission;
      sins of silence and complacency because of
        fear.
      Afraid, I sinned by waiting for a better
        moment
      to stand up for what I believe.
        Please forgive me.

Friday of the Fifth Week

Before he was assassinated, the saintly, martyred archbishop, Oscar Romero, spoke of the prophetic preaching against political oppression by a brother priest who was murdered by El Salvador's right-wing death squad. Romero said of him, "When Father Rafael Palacios was murdered in Saint Tecla and his body was laid out here, . . . he was still preaching!"

May these lenten days of the renewal of your baptism so permanently alter you as a witness of the gospel that at your wake, people will say of you what Romero said of Padre Rafael.

Rx: Preach the gospel without being ordained;
    Preach the gospel without a pulpit or
        words;
    Preach the gospel with your life as did
        Jesus.

Saturday of the Fifth Week

"The only sin," Martha Graham, the famous dancer and choreographer said, "is mediocrity!" In the book of Revelation the Cosmic Christ agrees with her: "Because you are lukewarm, neither hot nor cold, I will vomit you out of my mouth." If you've had a mediocre, tepid Lent, don't despair—it's not too late. Recall that Lent originally lasted only a week, so pledge to make next week the most prayerful seven days of your life. And let your lackluster Lent and past sins bring you closer to God, who agrees with the Russian writer Boris Pasternak, who said, "I don't like people who have never fallen or stumbled. Their virtue is lifeless and isn't of much value."

Rx: Passionate God,
   I am grateful for my lukewarm loving and
      sins,
   for all those times that I've stumbled and
      fallen,
   since wondrously all my trespasses have
      led me
   right into your heart, increasing your love
      for me.

Palm or Passion Sunday

Jesus was Easter absent-minded. Today begins the weeklong commemoration of Jesus' agonizing death without a trace of dread—because we know the last act! The Jesus riding into Jerusalem, eating at the Last Supper, and agonizing in Gethsemane, knew nothing of the last act—Easter. With death inescapable, he could only trust that his father in heaven would restore him to life, but he had no certainty that this would happen—no more than we do!

Rx: I believe in death, but confess I am an
     Easter agnostic;
  no atheist, but a doubter craving to
     comprehend Easter.
  So tattoo on my doubting heart,
     Beloved God,
       the words of St. Augustine,
  "Give me a lover, he will understand
     the resurrection."

Monday of Holy Week

God put a promise on Ezekiel's lips, "And you shall know that I am the LORD, when I open your graves, and bring you up. . . . I will put my spirit within you, and you shall live, . . . then you shall know that I, the LORD, have spoken and will act," (Ez 37:13–14).

Who trusts in the promise of a God whose very existence is questioned by endless centuries of war and the exploitation of the powerless by the greedy? Be patient and trust. You will be given infallible certitude of God's existence when the Spirit raises you out of your grave, for then "you shall know that I am the Lord!"

Rx: God of Endless Life,
    Bury me with all my doubts and
       fainthearted beliefs.
    But before I die, embalm me with a
       lover's conviction
    that upon awakening on my own Easter
       morning, I'll know you as:
       "I Am, I Have Been,
       and I'll Always Be."

Tuesday of Holy Week

Concerning this coming Good Friday, St. Paul wrote to us in his letter to the Philippians: "Let the same mind be in you that was in Christ Jesus, who, though he was in the form of God, emptied himself, taking the form of a slave . . . he humbled himself and became obedient to the point of death—even death on a cross" (Ph 2:5–8). Jesus emptied himself by becoming a "zero," the symbol for nothing, yet "nothing" is powerful.

In 1997, the computer that controlled the engines of the U.S.S. Yorktown erroneously attempted to divide by zero. The inability to perform such a mathematical impossibility caused the missile cruiser to be out of commission for three days! Do not be timid or retiring if you think of yourself as a "zero" in a world of very important people.

Rx: "Zero people" are not impotent;
    by being emptied
  they can be filled up with the Invisible
    Divine
  who longs to stall all the mighty engines of
    war.
  A zero is a halo, so wear yours with great
    dignity.

Wednesday of Holy Week

Lent began on a Wednesday and draws near its end on this Wednesday. Urban life will continue its headlong rush in the next holy days of this week, with all six lanes clogged bumper-to-bumper. The daily traffic of business, work, and entertainment floods our lives and our landscape. Holy Week is almost nonexistent or, at best, an endangered species outside of protected stained-glass sanctuaries. Yet this problem of being spiritually involved in the sacred mysteries of these days, while totally submerged in the mundane work-a-day world, isn't about Holy Week, but life itself. So in the coming days, take this prescription:

Rx: Daily, take the ancient medicine of
        remembering
     that Jerusalem's original holy week wasn't
        holy.
     There was nothing churchy about the Last
        Supper, the way of the cross,
        or the ugly death on Calvary.

     Yet in dirt, spit, and blood was hidden the
        sacred.
     Jesus knew that all of it was holy
        because he'd hallowed all the common,
        messy, pain of life.
     Holy Week challenges us to make every
        week holy.

These Three Days
The Triduum

Since ancient times, the three days from sundown on Holy Thursday through sundown on Easter Sunday have been called the Triduum. These holy days commemorating Jesus' Last Supper, his passion and death, his entombment, and his glorious resurrection mark the holiest days of our church year. They move us from the disciplines of Lent to the great fifty days of Easter rejoicing and new life. Continue your lenten renewal in these coming days of the Triduum, and be energized to live as a faithful disciple of Christ, born anew in Easter joy.

Holy Thursday
The Lord's Supper

John's gospel does not even mention the breaking of the bread at the Last Supper, but recounts instead how Jesus, like a slave, washed his disciples' feet. He then commanded them to be servant-slaves to each other. This servile washing of the feet is remembered ritually each year on Holy Thursday during the Mass of the Lord's Supper. But why only once a year? Shouldn't every celebration of the Lord's Supper ritually remember this most significant command of Jesus?

Every supper should be reverenced as a Last Supper. Every gathering at table with family or friends should be treasured because it may be the last! The menu for every meal should be the love of the Last Supper a love so generous as to want to give itself away, body and blood, for those who are present. Reverence every meal like the Last Supper since seated at every table is the Risen Christ alive in us. Christ delights in using our hands to lovingly serve others—not by washing feet, but by washing the dishes.

Rx: Use daily Jesus' favorite recipe for a Last Supper:
"Remember me as you pour and mix your love

into the bread, potatoes, and all that is
  served—
and into every deed or task of your
  hands."

Each day, carry out Jesus' last will and
  testament
by carrying out the trash, washing the
  dishes, and doing the laundry.
"Do these in memory of me, and be a
  servant to all,
for there is no greater love than to serve
  one another."

Good Friday
The Crucifixion and Death of Jesus

A radio reporter sent to New Jersey in 1937 to cover the landing of the famous German airship, *Hindenburg*, had no idea that he would witness a historic disaster. When the *Hindenburg* approached its landing tower, the giant dirigible suddenly exploded into enormous scarlet clouds of flames. As fire-engulfed bodies and debris fell from the sky, the radio reporter screamed, "Oh, the humanity!" Those listening to their radios were confused by his puzzling words, yet his spontaneous reaction was a primeval cry of anguish at the sight of his fellow humans dying in agony.

As you look at a crucifix or an image on television of someone dying, silently cry out that same primal prayer, "Oh, the humanity!" Not to feel distress and pain at the sight of brother and sister humans dying is to be diagnosed as soul dead.

Rx: To lack cognition is to be brain dead.
To lack compassion is to be soul dead.
Crucified Lord,
heal my heart, paralyzed by photographs,
so I can grieve every ugly Calvary I see.

Holy Saturday
The Day of the Tomb

Jesus made a tour of hell on this Saturday. As the Apostles' Creed says, "[he] . . . was crucified, died, and was buried. He descended into hell, and on the third day he arose again." While some versions of this prayer read "he descended to the dead," I prefer the original.

My old catechism said the hell Jesus visited wasn't the place of the damned, but rather a netherworld entombment of all since the time of Adam who had died after living a good life. Even in death Jesus proclaimed the good news, as the Baltimore catechism said, "His soul went down . . . to tell these good men [and women] that Heaven was now open to them, and that at his Ascension he would take them there with him."

Rx: Rejoice, you who are entombed in a living
          hell,
       your Savior comes to be with you in your
          torment.
       Regardless how hellish is your life or
          sickbed,
       he shares it and will return to take you to
          heaven.

Easter Sunday
The Feast of the Resurrection

In our culture, we speak of the deceased as "having departed," while in parts of Africa they say, "they have arrived." The difference is profound. This African expression challenges our idea of death as a thief who robs us of what is supposed to be ours forever. The great theologian of our times, Karl Rahner, said, "There are so many little deaths along the way, it doesn't matter which one is the last." In the same way, there are so many little resurrections along the way, it doesn't really matter which one is the last. Every little death is followed by a little Easter, and for every cross of Calvary there should be an Easter lily to carry.

Let this Easter Sunday be an Alleluia feast of remembrance of all your little resurrections so that you may live in abundant hope of your final, glorious resurrection.

Rx: The Creed of Easter People is in one
     word: "Alleluia!"
In the coming fifty days of Eastertide,
sprinkle it silently or aloud throughout
     your daily speech.
Greet the coming fifty sunrises with an
     "Alleluia,"

proclaim it at the sight of an empty
	parking space,
and sing it out as you drive past silent
	cemeteries.

Like a hello, "Alleluia" should joyously
	greet
every little resurrection after every little
	death,
as well as every solution to some
	seemingly dead-end dilemma.
Shout "Alleluia" as tulips bloom after
	winter,
as lovers kiss and make up after a quarrel,
or as old enemies agree to sign a peace
	treaty.

If, after Lent's forty days, your prayer
	pantry is bare
and your wine cellar of devotions dry,
just repeat over and over with intoxicating
	joy,
"Alleluia, Alleluia, Alleluia, Alleluia,
	Alleluia!"

Farewell Good News

Now that Lent is over, it isn't necessary to put away this little booklet of *prayscriptions* until next year. If the medicines in it have been helpful for the health of your soul and body, consider frequently referring back to this small booklet. For written on every *prayscription* is the option to "Refill as often as needed."

ABOUT THE AUTHOR

Edward Hays, author of over thirty books on contemporary spirituality has been a Catholic priest in the archdiocese of Kansas City, Kansas, since 1958. He has served as director of Shantivanam, a Midwest center of contemplative prayer, and as a chaplain of the state penitentiary in Lansing. He has spent extended periods of pilgrimage in the Near East, the Holy Land, and India. He continues his ministry as a prolific writer and painter in Leavenworth, Kansas.

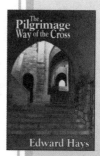